THE LITTLE BOOK OF
THE PROPERTIES OF MAGICAL ENERGY

ERIC & KATRINA RASBOLD

Copyright © 2013 Eric and Katrina Rasbold

2nd edition – 2014

3rd edition - 2016

All rights reserved.

Our beautiful cover artwork is compliments of fantasy artist, Janna Prosvirina. www.kuoma-stock.deviantart.com. Janna is both the photographer and the model.

ISBN: 1532863756
ISBN-13: 978-1532863752

CONTENTS

Introduction 1

Chapter 1 - How We Use Our Own Energy in the World..5

Chapter 2 - What Speeds Up and Facilitates Bio-Universal Energy?...10

Chapter 4 - What Slows Down Bio-Universal Energy Flow? 51

Chapter 5 – In Summary...66

About The Authors 70

Other Books by the Authors..72

Introduction

This book is part of the Bio-Universal Energy Series . Although it is intended to be used in conjunction with the other books in the series, the information that is contained within its pages can also stand alone by its own merit. You do not have to read the entire series to benefit from the lessons presented in each book.

Throughout this text, you will hear frequent mention of the term "Bio-Universal energy." This is a phrase we coined in our book *Energy Magic* to identify the merged process of "bio" energy (meaning your own personal energy and will that is inherent to YOU) and "universal" energy (meaning the energy of God, The Goddess, The Creator, The Universe – whatever you personally consider to be holy and sacred).

We believe that God takes on any number of forms and names to suit the comfort of each individual. The word "God" engenders visions of a being that is all-powerful and can therefore take on the appearance of any gender as well. It is only a word and by these terms that humankind has applied to The Divine, the term "Goddess" is just as valid as the word "God." Throughout this text, you will see many references to "God" and there is *no gender assignment* intended to this title. When you read "God," know that I am referring to the benevolent, all-knowing, omnipotent power that exists and is generally accepted as Deity. The words "Goddess," "The Universe," "The Divine," "Creator," etc, could just as easily be substituted and often will be.

The word "magic" is also frequently used in this book and it does not refer to the magic involved with stage illusion. The only similarity with stage magic is that something that was previously *there* is now *gone* or something that was not here before is now *here*. Within the context of this book, "magic" refers to the manifestation of positive change through the knowledge and use of Bio-Universal energy. When we think of magic in this sense, it becomes an acronym that means:

"**M**ake **A** **G**enerative and **I**nteresting **C**hange."

When our lives take us to a place that is lacking peace and prosperity and we are in need of help, we seek change. Why even bother if the change we make is not generative and interesting? One of the most fundamental aspects of any spiritual path is the premise that if we connect with our chosen deity and ask for help, assistance will be given by that process. The use of Bio-Universal energy explores that process to a greater degree and gives one a deeper understanding of the nature of spiritual connection. Bio-Universal energy work utilizes the basic principles of physics, which applies what we know about mundane physical energy to the use of spiritual energy.

For instance, we now know by way of the Law of Conservation of Energy that we can neither create nor destroy energy; we can only convert it into something else. It is important to understand that energy is not "conjured" or called into existence by some arcane method of wizardry. It must be "drawn" or raised from a source within or without the body, mind, or soul. This tells us that in order to use our Bio-Universal energy effectively, we must harness it and cause it to become what we will it to be. It *wants* to change into something observable. The energy *wants* to become "generative and interesting." The trick comes in knowing how to do so in a way that is positive and responsible.

Beginning with *Energy Magic*, we, the authors, initiated a study of how to combine our own personal energy with that of The Divine to create positive life change. Too often, we are instructed to pray for what we want, but we are not told *how* to pray. In the Bible, Jesus gives us specific instructions for how to do so, but it is limited to the recitation of the Lord's Prayer. There is no direction on what we should feel when we pray or how we should direct our internal energy.

In nature-based religious practices, we are often told to do this spell work or read this part of a ritual, but here again we are not told how we should feel or what connections we should make. In the Bio-Universal Energy Series, we explore many ways to join your energy with Universal energy and to direct it toward a specific goal that needs attention in your life.

For a much more detailed examination of the foundations, concepts and methods of the use of Bio-Universal energy, *The Little Book of Reuniting the Two Selves*, explores at length what exactly Bio-Universal energy is, where it comes from, and how the energy centers in our bodies move it through us, as well as how blockages of our energy flow can affect us.

By popular request, some of our best-selling e-books in the Bio-Universal Energy Series are now translating out into print form in the "Little Book of..." series.

In this book, *The Little Book of The Properties of Magical Energy,* we extensively address what speeds up your Bio-Universal energy and what slows it down. It is possibly one of the most dynamic books in the Bio-Universal Energy Series because it takes a detailed look at what factors and practices speed up your Bio-Universal energy flow and which ones slow it down or even ground it completely.

Chapter 1 - How We Use Our Own Energy in the World

The study of Bio-Universal energy and its use in creating the life we want to live is one that never ends. Not only do we continually discover new and interesting ways to apply Bio-Universal energy in our own lives, but also the ever-evolving field of study regarding energy itself constantly creates new knowledge of how energy of all kinds works. We can usually apply these newly emerging principles to Bio-Universal energy as well. Keep the theories and "facts" (and the fact is that "facts" constantly change in the scientific world) that you learned in high school Earth Sciences in mind as we explore the principles of Bio-Universal energy and you will quickly see that what applies to one type of energy, applies to another as well.

Just because we have not yet learned to measure and directly observe the movement of Bio-Universal energy does not mean it does not exist. Did atoms not exist before we developed the technology to see and purposefully manipulate them? Did air only begin to exist when we could determine what elements came together to create it? No, atoms and air were there even before we could define them. Could we touch the items that are made of atoms and could we breathe before we knew what was in air? Most certainly. Just like air and atoms, the fact that we have not yet developed the technology to conduct a full, formal study of Bio-Universal energy does not prevent us from enjoying the benefits of its existence.

Until that time does come, we can be confident that Bio-Universal energy responds to some of the same factors as other types of known and studied energy in our lives. As you learn more about using Bio-Universal energy to create positive life changes and construct the life you want to live, you will begin to see how much Bio-Universal energy mirrors electricity and other forms of energy that we take for granted in our physical world. Our understanding of energy as a whole and its assigned scientific principles guide us in the appropriate and successful use of Bio-Universal energy.

Try to retrain your mind to consider the spiritual energy that is processed through your chakra system, transported through your meridian system, then cleansed and purified by your lymphatic system as *actual energy,* just like electricity. Remember the law of energy conservation: *"Energy cannot be created or destroyed; only converted from one form to another."*

When you are born, you have a soul/spirit. That spirit has energy that is your own personal "bio" energy. The energy naturally seeks to change into form and manifest in other ways. You release energy as a baby when you cried and that energy created a reaction in other people that we hope resulted in someone feeding you or nurturing you in some other necessary way. You expended energy and garnered a desired reaction from the other energies around you.

This is the rudimentary beginning of a lifetime of energy expression and usage. As you grow, the use of your personal energy to get what you want in life is tremendously refined through the conditioning and learning processes. Through feedback from the world around you, you develop a sense of when it is appropriate to use your energy to get what you want and when it is not. You wait until after your mother is off the phone to ask for a cookie. You take turns playing with a toy you love because you have learned to share and be kind. As you continually refine the ways you use your energy in your life, you learn particular modifying behaviors that allow you to get what you want faster, such as social cues like the words "Please," and "May I?" You learn that there is an element of timing to the use of your energy and that you will be more successful at getting what you want if you ask at the right time or on the right day. For example, a young boy will learn that Dad is more likely to fix the bike on the weekend rather than on a weekday immediately after he returns home from work.

A successful adult has usually mastered all or most of the cues of knowing when to push forward with their energy towards what they want and when to wait or even withdraw their energy completely. An imbalance in that scale invariably leads to a socially dysfunctional person. On one side, you have the lethargic, fearful, apathetic person who resists any change and refuses to use their own energy to make their life better. On the other side, you have an overly ambitious, cutthroat workaholic who will take advantage of anyone to get what they want in life.

In the use of Bio-Universal energy work, not only do we strive for the perfect balance between those two extremes, but we also learn to channel our "bio" energy, which is the physical and tangible energy described in the explanations above, and combine it with "universal" energy to accentuate our output and achieve our goals faster. We also cultivate a familiarity and closeness with our overall life plan and "Greatest Good" so that the goals we seek to achieve are also those endorsed by The Universe. We trust in "The Process" and make every effort to coordinate our own desires with what the Universe identifies as our life's mission.

We become more keenly aware of what opens our lives to joy and fulfillment, not only through an understanding of our life's mission, but also by knowing ourselves fully and being free from social delusion and masks. It becomes increasingly apparent what behaviors and situations need to be cultivated in our lives and which ones we need to eliminate. We become so invested in the wonderful life we are crafting that we no longer have interest in the behaviors and influences that bring drama, worry, energy drain, and fear into our thought matrix.

This is, of course, not an immediate result, but one that develops over time as a person becomes more in tune with the will of God in their life and their own needs and wants. It also enacts a way that is neither harmful nor destructive. Once we relax into the flow that is already at work in our lives, these influences tend to fall away, leaving us free to direct the flow of our ever-increasing rush of personal and Divine energy toward the goals we wish to manifest.

With that being the case, it is important to know how that energy flow reacts to different influences. Sometimes, the simplest shifts in behavior, environment, or even thoughts, can significantly affect our natural energy flow.

Chapter 2 - What Speeds Up and Facilitates Bio-Universal Energy?

As with electricity and other forms of energy, when we are working with Bio-Universal energy, there are conductors and there are resistors that affect the circuit and flow of energy. Certain factors that will speed it up and help it move faster and others will slow it down or ground it. We can use the knowledge of these properties to direct, intensify, and speed up our spiritual connection. If we want to move electricity, we can use a conductor such as a metal or water mixed with an electrolyte because we know it to be energy receptive and directive. If we do not want electricity to move, we use a grounding agent such as earth, rubber, or other materials, that stop the flow. It is the same with Bio-Universal energy. There are conductors and there are resistors. Knowing what those are and how they work is necessary to create the most positive outcome from our energy work.

We have all used a telephone with a "bad" connection. "Can you hear me now?" is probably one of the most commonly used phrases on a cell phone. We repeat ourselves, move to different areas, or even try phoning back again with hope of getting a better connection. The connection itself exists, but we cannot get our thoughts conveyed because of interference of one kind or another on the line. The goal with using Bio-Universal energy is to create an environment and mindset where our calls go right through every time and are loud, crisp, and clear. We want to amplify the energy we direct toward a goal to and move it quickly toward its target.

Some people refer to this process as "magic," because it works like magic. From thoughts and words, form becomes manifest. Just like a magician on a stage who pulls something from nowhere, so do we manifest a positive outcome purely from our connection to God. Throughout our books, you will often hear our instructors use the term "magic" or "magical work" in reference to Bio-Universal energy work.

The explanation we like best for the word "magic" in this:

Make A Generative and Interesting Change

The operative words here are, of course, "generative" which means to have the power or the function of generating, originating, producing, or reproducing, and "interesting" because if it's boring, who cares?

Every time we pray, we change our lives in some way. If we do not get what we want, we learn that what we want was not in the interest of our greatest good. If what we want happens, we have changed our lives through the generative nature of our prayers answered. Regardless, change occurs, either in our knowledge and understanding or through manifestation in the outside world. Our goal is to make that change something lovely and interesting. Prayer is one way of connecting to God and sending energy toward a goal. It is one of the ways to use Bio-Universal energy.

There are very specific ways of praying. By "praying," we mean engaging God/Goddess in a meaningful way that will convey our intentions clearly. Of course, God understands our hearts and what we want to do and say. The Lord loves drunks, little children, and people who struggle with words and intent. It is for *our own benefit* that we must be as specific as possible.

The "universal" part of "Bio-Universal" is completely aware of what we wish to accomplish before we even ask. The "bio" part has to engage both the Higher Self and the Conscious Self and get both of those two feisty horses to pull the cart in the right direction. If you are interested in more information on the Higher Self and the Conscious Self, you may want to read our book, *The Little Book of Reuniting the Two Selves,* which covers this subject in detail. The following factors can greatly assist our own Higher Self in relating to our Conscious Self to get them on the same page and working together effectively toward our goals.

The Impact of Ritual

Ritual is a word that many people shy away from thinking it is about congress with the devil. Saying that you are "getting ready to have a ritual" sounds sinister and spooky. A ritual is nothing more than a specific set of actions, performed for their symbolic value to affect a desired outcome. Often, it represents a behavior that we repeat throughout life. When a Christian congregation sings the Doxology or passes the offering plate, that is a ritual. When you blow out the candles on your birthday cake or put a star on top of the Christmas tree, that is a ritual. The words "ritual" and "tradition" are beautifully interconnected.

The sole purpose of ritual is to focus our intent and our energy, so it is an important part of our Bio-Universal energy techniques. In ritual, there is a specific flow and procedure and every act becomes deliberate and meaningful. As the definition implies, there is a great deal of symbolism to your actions when working in ritual. The Higher Self, which is our own spiritual pathway, responds favorably to symbolism, so ritual is a means to access the place where God speaks to us. That is why most religious ceremony is rife with ritual. The procedure of ritual itself works to take us into Higher Self.

Very nearly every time we work with Bio-Universal energy, we will perform a ritual of some kind. Ritual is very personal and adaptable. There is no hard and fast set of rules for how you conduct your own ritual, despite the attempts of many religious groups over the centuries to insist on particular "rule." Our book *The Little Book of The Art of Ritual Crafting* focuses specifically on how to construct an effective and meaningful ritual in which to practice Bio-Universal (or other magical) energy work.

The act of ritual tells our Conscious Self to relax and make room for the Higher Self to share our time. Ritual tells us that we are not performing a mundane activity, but are instead engaging the sacred and spiritual moments in our lives. This acts as a trigger in sensory perception, mood, and mindset that amplifies our own bio-energy output and causes us to be more receptive to universal energy flow. When you choose certain actions that allow you to be in connection with God/Goddess/The Universe such as lighting incense, relaxing your body, meditating, playing specific music that puts you in the right frame of mind, lighting candles, and such energy focusing activities, you are creating a ritual. It is strongly advised that all Bio-Universal energy work be enacted in the context of some form of ritual in order to give it the most sacred and holy framework that you are able to create for performing your work. Can you work energy magic on the fly and in the moment? Absolutely, although it is not as easy to do so for beginners as it is for practitioners who have a great deal of experience in formal ritual crafting and still, the energy will be intensified if ritual is actually used.

How Color Affects Bio-Universal Energy

The human mind reacts automatically to certain colors and we can use this knowledge to create a particular mood and amplify the energy we generate toward our goal. Colors are a powerful tool to use when we are generating and directing Bio-Universal energy.

One of the primary tenets of the use of Bio-Universal energy is finding the ways in which our Conscious Self and our Higher Self can connect and communicate. Our book called *The Little Book of Reuniting of the Two Selves* discusses at length the importance of reconnecting the Conscious Self with the Higher Self in order to maximize the flow of Bio-Universal energy and achieve greater results.

Because God/Goddess/The Universe communicates with us through the Higher Self, it is essential that we work on an ongoing basis to keep that Higher Self engaged and active at all times. We can achieve improved communication between the two selves through spoken language, but the most direct and fluid communication comes through the non-word interactions of symbolism and color. Before delving into a discussion of the use of color, it is very important to understand that color is a specific frequency of light. Light is pure energy, and as such, color itself is a specific *type of energy.*

Interestingly enough, the Higher Self and the Universe often speak *back to us* through colors. Have you ever found that yourself unexpectedly drawn to certain jewelry, stones, or clothes of a particular color when you had no attraction to them before? This is our connection to the Divine telling us that we need to build up a particular frequency of energy in our lives. I, for instance, used to wear the color black almost exclusively. In retrospect, I see that this was during a time when I wanted to hide away from society and act as an invisible part of the world. Black cloaked me from interaction with others, even though that was not a clothing color choice that I made consciously with that motive in mind. Now, I prefer deep jewel tones in clothing colors and, in keeping with the premise, I now live a very vibrant, full, and social life invested in energy and personal strength. My color choices changed when my personal motives changed and neither time was it a conscious choice.

Colors create a visceral, psychological reaction in humans that affect us every single day. The use of colors in advertising, architecture, therapy, teaching, and decorating is as much a part of our society as the use of verbal language. We use colors to create a specific reaction in people and we use the energy of that reaction to enhance and strengthen our Bio-Universal energy flow.

Individually and as a species, colors trigger feelings and feelings are the true root of the "bio" part of "Bio-Universal" energy. It is through our feelings that our own energy takes shape and begins to flow. Anger, love, excitement, fear, tranquility, guilt... they all have their own flavor and effect within us. The energy of that sensation is extremely recognizable and fluid; therefore, like any other energy, we can direct it.

Sometimes, our own experiences as individuals condition our feelings about colors affect our reactions. If you mother made you dress in pink for your entire grade school experience, for instance, you might carry with you a very negative reaction to the color, especially if you happen to be male gendered. Our culture also conditions us into certain beliefs about colors, such as "pink is for girls and blue is for boys." The color yellow is often associated with cowardice and green is associated with envy. These associations are specific to cultural conditioning, yet are almost as valid as our natural reactions we generate from inside rather than outside.

On a deeper level, people react to certain color schemes on a subconscious level. This is why you will rarely see a prison or a hospital painted red or yellow. Both red and yellow are very stimulating, excitable colors and more suited for restaurants or stadiums where the designers want to elicit a hyperactive, enthusiastic reaction. Mint greens, pastel blues, and soft earth tones are calming and used more often in facilities dedicated toward healing and creating a tranquil atmosphere.

The colors themselves become the symbolic pathway into the Higher Self to create a particular feeling resulting from the inherent physical energy vibration of the color. The "programming" of our conscious thought is circumnavigated and we are hard-wired to respond to different colors in particular ways, despite our cultural, external conditioning. This premise is the foundation of the color associations of the Chakras, or energy centers within the human body.

The chakra points in our bodies are energy centers that generate a tremendous amount of bio energy. The energy at each point has attributes that are specific to their location. Each of the seven primary chakras has its own color affiliation directly associated with the inherent energy properties of that particular color.

How can we use this knowledge to increase the flow of Bio-Universal energy? There are several ways, actually. The most obvious is to surround ourselves, both in wardrobe and interior design, with colors that support and create the feelings we want to have play a dominant role in our lives. You might choose particular colors for the rooms in your home based on their intended purpose. You could dress in certain colors that support a goal you have for the day. Colored accents in your environment can create a focus that you want to enhance. For instance, you might have a room that is decorated in earthy tones to create a peaceful, grounded atmosphere, but have red accents to create little energy pulses throughout the décor.

I have seen this particular usage of color at work with children, in fact. If you have a child who has difficulty sleeping, cannot seem to focus, or has any kind of attention deficit issues or behavioral problems, you would not want to have their bedroom painted in stimulating colors. If you want a warm and hospitable feeling in your family room, you would not use stark blacks or whites as your color scheme. I am sure that as you consider the applications of this idea, you can imagine limitless ways you can speak to your Higher Self through color use.

When you are specifically directing energy toward a goal, you want to surround yourself with colors that support that goal. Any candles or stones you use should be of what we call a "sympathetic" color, meaning that it encourages the specific energy flow you want to achieve. Many people use an altar cloth to decorate their workspace and that should be of a color that compliments your objective for that ritual.

Because we use candles for extended release of stored Bio-Universal energy, it is particularly important that you choose a color that relates well to your goal. White, it is important to note, is a universal color and we may use it in place of any other color in a pinch. The reason that white can serve for any purpose is because the color of white contains ALL frequencies of light and thereby actually contains ALL colors. Choosing the right color for your candle work is a big step toward increasing the energy the candle will absorb and then later release.

Colors In Relation to Chakra Points In Your Body

Before you begin doing your energy work toward a specified goal, it can help to "wake up" the chakra areas that relate to what you are doing.

To ignite the power of a specific chakra, close your eyes and envision the area of your body where that particular chakra is located flooded with its associated color. Do this for a minimum of four or five minutes and then proceed with your energy work. In the case of color work, you can choose the chakra work that is associated with the color that vibrates on the frequency for the Bio-Universal energy work you want to do and it is very likely that you will automatically select the appropriate chakra point.

As you review the particular energies inherent in each of the colors below, always remember that your own personal experiences may have created other filters that affect the way you naturally react to a particular color. Your own reactions will be the result of a combination of natural and conditioned responses. We fully recommend using the color chart below to boost your energy flow when channeling and directing Bio-Universal energy.

Energy Associations of Colors

White – Spirituality, cleansing, purity, perfection,

innocence, integrity, healing, freedom, opportunity, forgiveness, and acceptance. White is also a color of simple power and may traditionally be used to substitute for any other color. Because it reflects and radiates, white will also enhance the power of other color magic in Bio-Universal energy work. It eliminates negative energy and creates inner peace. It also corresponds to the Maiden aspect of the Goddess archetypes and because of its association with purity, is the color of candles often used in orthodox church services.

Black – Death, the Underworld, grounding, stability, mystery and magic. The primary purpose of the color black is to absorb negative energy and minimizing the effect of other particular energies such as pulling in energy you want to erase, for instance. Whereas white is projective and radiates energy outward, black absorbs and grounds energy into itself and downward. Black corresponds to the Crone aspect of the Goddess archetypes.

Red – Element of Fire, **the Root Chakra**, the God Ares, Mars, love, passion, sex, self-confidence, success, strength, creativity, persistence, energy, and vitality. Red is excellent for energy work to draw in love, passion, creativity and urgent healing spells. Red is associated with the Root Chakra and with powerful emotion, so it is an excellent color to use for emergencies that require intense energy and quick results. Red corresponds to the Mother aspect of the Goddess archetypes.

Pink – Love from the heart, nurturing, tenderness, sensitivity, harmony, femininity, and innocence. While red is associated with fiery love and passion, pink corresponds to the gentler aspects of these emotions. Pink is also good for energy work involving skin health and recovery from wounds. Pink is a tint and is therefore, very close in the color spectrum to white, which lends the purity aspect to the color.

Orange – The Sacral (Navel) Chakra, harvest time, happiness, excitement, assertiveness, motivation, persistence, and prosperity. Orange is a very motivating color and is great for eliminating procrastination, lethargy, anxiety, and stress. It is also helpful when trying to create solutions or new ways of accomplishing your goals. Orange helps us to get moving and to create positive change. Orange increases self-confidence and sense of capability. It is the perfect blend of the passion of red with the power of yellow.

Yellow – The Solar Plexus Chakra, the Sun and Sun God(s), joy, cheerfulness, intellect, hope, direction, personal power, clear thinking, concentration, fruitfulness, and communication. Interestingly enough, while cowardly people are often described as "yellow," the color is actually great for banishing fear and treachery. This is particularly true for bright yellows. In essence, it seeks out courage from within a person and brings that quality forward. The Sun is the most powerful astrological symbol and has been worshipped for years and its primary color association is yellow. When a child draws a sun, they will typically color it yellow. The Sun is a masculine symbol and so all of the male characteristics of bravery, strength, power, protectiveness and the warrior spirit are associated with yellow. You can see from their inherent energies why red and yellow are such excitable colors.

Green – The Heart Chakra, the Earth Goddess, the Element Earth, the forests, nature, nature, wealth, abundance, longevity, and healing. Green is used in energy work for healing, grounding, establishing stability, and for drawing in wealth and prosperity. Green and gold are the colors of our money because the energy of wealth is already within the colors! Green and blue are the colors of the earth when we view it from above, so both are powerful healing colors. Most herbs are green or brown when dried which contributes to the healing aspects of the color.

Blue – The Throat Chakra, the Element Water, communication, creativity, integrity, calmness, truth, loyalty, justice, leadership and clear thinking. It is said that a lie cannot be maintained while a blue candle burns. Blue "balances the scales" and equalizes debts. "True Blue" is a phrase that comes from the loyalty aspect of the color and "Blue Blood" denotes royalty, which brings with it an association (possibly unearned) of leadership and integrity. Blue is very calming and tranquil, thanks to our blue oceans, seas, and lakes and the negative ions they emit. Interestingly enough, the color blue is associated with the Element Silver. This noble metal is the most reflective of all known substances – and therefore perfectly reflects the truth back to the observer. The ingestion of this metal from silver crafted utensils is the cause of a phenomenon known as agyria in which the silver actually tints the skin from within the body an irrevocable shade of blue and is the source of the term "blue-blood." As only the exceedingly wealthy could afford silver utensils, this phenomenon became associated with royalty and other persons of high status.

Indigo - The Brow (or Pineal, or Third Eye) Chakra, idealism, justice, wisdom, inspiration, intuition, spirituality, psychic powers and the understanding of things. We use indigo in Bio-Universal energy work to help reduce phobias and stress, as well as seeking out one's Higher Self and connectivity to Deity and other benevolent energies. You will notice that the higher we go up the colors of the chakra spectrum, the more esoteric and ethereal the color associations become. This is because we are moving further up the body to the locations where the Higher Self tends to hang out. The colors progressively increase in frequency and are therefore "finer" manifestations of energy. Indigo is a color that is not often used in its purest form. It amplifies the power of blue to "balance the scales" and can invoke or balance karma. Be careful when you invoke karma, however. It tends to get messy. In our book *The Little Book of Magical Ethics and Protection,* we delve into the role of karma and ways to avoid karmic backlash.

Violet or Purple - The Crown Chakra, inspiration, spirituality, the sacred, selflessness, tolerance, intuition, imagination, royalty, wealth, inner peace, security, protection, creativity, freedom, and personal responsibility. We use purple in energy work for protection and psychic ability. It generates results that are "the highest and the best," which may or may not produce the result you seek. Higher Self, because it combines with Universal energy and is our conduit to the Divine, views our lives on a broader scale than we are able to see. For that reason, when you use a high-level color such as purple, you tend to bring into play, even more so than with other colors and intentions, the aspect of what you NEED rather than what you WANT. Ultimately, this invariably works out better for us in the end, but in the moment, ego can sometimes take over when things do not manifest as we expect. Purple is long associated with wealth because the dyes used to create purple came from very expensive sources and were often only available to royalty. Violet is a very protective color.

Other colors not used to represent chakra energy centers, but often used in magical workings are the following:

Brown – Grounding, good health, hard work, stability, reward from effort, and element of Earth. Brown is, as you can imagine, a very earthy color and is related to "people of the earth." Most non-dyed materials used for weaving clothing were off white or brown, so it is a color that is associated with a certain type of closeness to hard work and effort whereas purple is the color for royalty. Brown is great for generating energy that is associated with personal accomplishment from your own efforts. It is a workhorse color and lends its uncommon strength to any other colors you choose to use. That is why the color brown goes with almost every other color from a decorative standpoint. Brown is also associated with creation and growth. Clay that comes from the ground is brown or brownish-red and we can mold it into whatever the artist desires. The crops that provide our sustenance come from the body of the brown earth. No matter who you are, from the lowest pauper to the highest king, you likely eat something every day that births from our Mother Earth's brown bosom.

Gold – The Sun, masculine energy, success, money, abundance, power, positivity, confidence, self-motivation, self-discipline, generosity, enlightenment, and manifestation. The color is very useful in energy work that focuses on success, wealth, and self-confidence. Fool's Gold (Iron Pyrite) has this power, despite of the negativity of the name, and works well for drawing in wealth. Gold is appealing, shiny, a little ostentatious, and reflects the light very well. It has worth that transcends any economic state, so it is a color of tremendous endurance and versatility. Gold is valued so highly because it is the only substance known to humans that is indestructible. Neither time, nor rust, nor moth shall corrupt it; it is the only physical object truly considered 'eternal.'

Silver – The Moon, feminine energy, balance, harmony, change, learning, introspection, confidence, wealth, secrets, healing, hidden desires, and intuition. Silver is very useful in divination and meditation. It is also useful for tapping into and increasing your psychic power and/or intuition. On occasion, silver is used for money drawing energy work. Silver is mysterious and introspective. Only recently have we begun to explore the healing properties of and are tremendous. Silver is associated often with mirrors, so the color can be used to get in touch with your real self and for personal introspection.

Grey – Used to work through morning, sorrow, humility, doubt, and uncertainty. It is also good for obscuring what you do not want to have seen; "a grey area," and for creating confusion. If you want to hide something, put grey energy all around it or slip a representation of that hidden object, like words written on a slip of paper, into a grey bag and hide it from view.

As you can see, there are many uses for color in your Bio-

Universal energy work. Each color will speak to you on a very personal level if you will open yourself to its individual energy. Harnessing that feeling that is created in you and in others by the various colors in our world is an excellent way to connect with your Higher Self and let it know your goals and desires.

Herbs and Scents

Many spiritual paths have used smoldering herbs, resins, roots, essential oils, and incenses throughout recorded history. There is little doubt that the sense of smell is one of the most powerful mood setters in existence for humans. The smell of bread baking, chocolate, freshly cut grass, certain colognes or after shave, and other personal olfactory triggers will quickly carry you to a particular mindset and activate stored memories faster than any other method.

We have known for thousands of years that certain smells create specific reactions in humans. Aromatherapy did not exist by that name even a hundred years ago, yet humans knew that they could burn items to create scent and use the power of the scent to elicit a specific set of physical or emotional responses. A French chemist named Rene-Maurice Gattefosse coined the word 'aromatherapy' in 1937, then an French Army surgeon named Jean Valnet pioneered the use of essential oils in the late 1940s. In recent years, the understanding of the effect scents have on our bodies and minds has greatly affected how we practice healing and live our lives.

Our reaction to scent in ritual is both physical and emotional. If your mother ever rubbed your chest with a Vapor-rub when you were little, the smell of eucalyptus may be especially soothing to you now when you have a cold and will automatically activate healing energies inside you and instantly open you more fully to any healing energy that is sent to you or cultivated around you. There is a physical reaction because eucalyptus has the healing property of opening up the sinuses and promoting drainage. There is also an emotional reaction from the nostalgic memory of the protection and comfort from your mother. In Bio-Universal energy work, we work with both reactions as they come, the intrinsic and the personal, and optimize the choice of herbs based on our own emotional reaction and the properties that are naturally inherent to the scent of the plant.

When you set the atmosphere for your ritual space, there are many ways you can create a pleasing scent that promotes your goals:

Incense – There are many, many incenses available on the market and most are relatively inexpensive. Incense can be handmade or purchased as sticks, cones, or powders.

Resins – Copal, amber, frankincense, and myrrh are among the resins that can be burned on small, round, self-igniting charcoal briquettes. ***This is a different kind of charcoal briquette than the ones you use in your barbeque grill.*** BBQ charcoals are NOT for indoor use! The correct ones for inside use look like these:

These types of briquettes continually spark after you light them, so they constantly reignite themselves. You can burn powdered incenses, herbs, scented oils, or resins on them very effectively.

Scented candles - Some candles have a strong scent pitch and can provide a pleasing aroma for your ritual area.

Oils – There are two kinds of oils fur use in magical workings. There are essential oils which are pure oils extracted from the source plant matter and there are scented oils which are the essential oils placed in carrier oil like grape seed oil or sweet almond oil. Essential oils are usually more expensive, but last longer because they are not cut with a carrier oil. Either works well as long as you have a good, organic oil without chemical fillers, which can cause headaches in some people.

Potpourri – Potpourri is a collection of fragrant herbs, oils, and spices that you placed out on their own or cover with boiling water in a burner of some type. Their scent will carry on the steam that releases from the heat.

If, for instance, you wanted to create a healing ritual for a friend who is ill, you might use a eucalyptus-based scent to increase the healing energy around you and through you before directing the energy to the one who is sick. If you are working to bring love into your life, you could use a rose scent to evoke that energy. If you wanted to attract money to you, you would use a spice-based scent. There are several books and references on the market that will educate you at length what scents are appropriate for specific goals.

The second use of herbs and flowers in ritual is for a visual effect. A flower bouquet is a lovely addition to the altar area for a spring ritual to welcome the warmer temperatures. Harvest altars often have wheat or corn on them. Plants and herbs serve as living imagery to assist with the evocation of specific feelings in accordance with the type of energy you wish to create.

Yet another use lies in the medicinal property of the herb

or flower itself; a concept that has long been known by folk magic practitioners and the physiological efficacy of which is finally starting to be acknowledged by the mainstream scientific world.

Sound

The use of various sounds and music in ritual is very nearly universal throughout spiritual paths. Most religions have their own preferred music and sounds for different effects. This is also a highly individualized field. You may hear people say, "My feet just won't behave!" when they hear a particular song. We hear a song from our past and we temporarily transported back in time. A particularly poignant song can have us in tears or a happy one can compel us to dance. An old adage says "music soothes the savage beast." This is because music speaks not only to our Conscious Self, but also to our Higher Self. Music is one of those shared languages that can bridge the gap between the two selves and bring them together in communion.

There is little denying that music and sound are powerful factors that affect our mood, mindset, and our ability to focus. Some people enjoy chanting, some like heavy percussion, others like techno, and some like New Age music. Some people like to do their spiritual work in complete silence. There is no "wrong" choice of sound. You can play recorded music or create your own for your magical work. You can softly beat on a drum and meditate to the entrancing sound. The sounds around you during spiritual work create an emotional impact and affect your own energy movement and direction. It would not be ideal, for instance, to do our spiritual work while a car alarm is going off a few feet away from us or a dog is barking incessantly.

Take some time – and perhaps a trip through YouTube.com – to gauge your reaction to different types of sounds. You will find music that soothes you, music that builds excitable energy, and music that you never want to hear again. Music and sounds are major mood setters and the energy of the mood they create is yet another piece of the Bio-Universal energy puzzle that can contribute additional energy and force to your flow.

Entering Trance State

Like the word "ritual," "trance" is a word that has gotten a very bad reputation. Trancing is a type of meditation in which you respond to music, activity, or other stimulation in such a way that you enter into an altered state. Your visual stimulation might begin to fade away as you go further inside your own mind during the trance. Far from losing control of your mind (which seems to be the baseless fear most people associate with the practice), you are actually more in control of your mind and can very easily access Higher Self. A person can achieve a trance state through many methods, but the most common are dancing, fire gazing, drumming, chanting, humming, listening to music, and meditating.

A trance state is not usually something that happens to a person right away or to a novice. "Talking in tongues," which is a practice common to Pentecostal religions, is a form of trance. Some deep meditations qualify as trances. Some people who pray the rosary, a Catholic practice, may pray themselves into a trance. Trances are common in situations of sensory deprivation. They sometimes take place in sweat lodges of Native American practices. The basic common experience with trancing is that what is around you in your sensory perception fades and you begin to have an altered perception. This is not usually a drug-induced experience. Properly done, this can result in a near perfect communion with your Higher Self. It is about complete and total focus on the interior to the full exclusion of the exterior. Since mastery of this practice fully engages Higher Self, it is the spiritual equivalent of getting the number to the Bat phone and is often the ultimate goal of the serious magical practitioner.

The Spoken and the Written Word

Humans often consider the power of speech and written word to be the defining quality that sets us apart from the rest of the animal world. Although some animals have been trained through extensive teaching to communicate (Koko the Gorilla, for instance), as far as evidence shows, humans alone possess the ability to avail themselves of effective communication through the spoken and/or the written language. Much like our Bio-

Universal energy, we can use language to hurt and we can use it to help. Words have varying degrees of power depending on their application.

There is little denying the power of words. For something used so often and so carelessly, we do take them very seriously. We all have memories of times when words cut us to the bone and left us to bleed. A theory states that it takes 100 positive words to make up for one negative one. Sometimes, words imprint on our psyches to the point that they become the filter through which we experience our lives. Damage that changes our lives forever happens through words and the interesting part is that the person doing the wounding may have no idea they have hurt us or changed us in some significant way. They may never know that they held the sword that dealt our self-confidence a fatal blow.

Likewise, hearing positive, uplifting words can bring our whole day into the sunlight. We thrive on hearing good things about ourselves and the experience can dramatically change our attitudes. Words can give us a completely new perspective when nothing else will do the job. Words are power and when you learn to use your words to support your goals, you have tapped into a tremendous energy accelerator.

The power of words varies depending on the form they take. The written word is very solid, substantial, and provable, but it lacks inflection and intonation, which are a big part of human communication. On the other hand, the spoken word is fleeting, subjective, and fickle. "That's not what we said" or, "That's not what we meant" have to be the most frequently used phrases known to humankind. Unless a conversation is tape recorded, words that are spoken are often twisted and misconstrued and not always with malice.

When a message is in print, however, it is provable. The context and inflection is up for debate, but the words themselves are there in black and white. This is why written contracts and words are admissible in court proceedings and hearsay is not.

Thought, on the other hand, is the most insubstantial form of wording. Our thoughts, to steal a metaphoric phrase, "tumble in our heads, making and breaking alliances like underpants in a tumble dryer." Our thoughts certainly have power; often more than we know. Thoughts are the seeds from which all form manifests and generally precede all spoken words or actions.

Once you turn your thoughts into words, spoken or written, their power increases tremendously. You may have heard the phrase, "You can't un-ring the bell." Once we say something aloud, it we cannot un-say it. Hurtful words, for instance, can deeply scar us. The person who offended us can apologize with the most sincere, articulate, emotional apology imaginable and offer up all of the right reasons for why they said something so hurtful. We can forgive them, move on, and have a positive relationship with them. We will always know, however, that they are capable of saying hurtful, horrible things. We may convince ourselves that they will not do it again, but the knowledge that they are capable of doing so never, ever goes away. It is the bell we cannot un-ring. Words can have an irrevocable once they stop rattling around in your head and exit by way of mouth or pen.

Words have a hierarchy of impact in power. From least to greatest:

1 - Words that are still only thoughts

2- The spoken word

3- The written word

4 - Written words that are spoken aloud

5 - Written words that are spoken loud in front of others (witnesses)

6 - Written words that are spoken aloud repeatedly (chanting or affirmations)

We can use this hierarchy of power in our Bio-Universal energy work by affirming our goals and intentions in both the written and spoken word. Certainly, we can pray in our heads and we can work magic in our heads without saying or writing a word. It is not a matter of such an act being impossible, but more that there is a greater impact when the words are spoken aloud or written down.

Speaking our will aloud and in some cases, speaking it aloud repeatedly such as through affirmations, accentuates the flow of energy toward a particular goal. As we say a phrase repeatedly, we naturally lend accent to different parts of the phase or sentence. This causes us to consider the phrase or sentence differently and internalize the information on a different level.

Some people who work with esoteric energy enjoy using ancient languages. The Jewish faith uses the Hebrew language when they read the Torah and the Catholic faith uses Latin for some of their recitations. Most Christian Bible readings are in the linguistic form of the time in which they were written rather than in our own modern way of speaking. Each of these spiritual paths assigns great power to the strength of the spoken and written word. Some magical paths appreciate the use of systems such as the Theban alphabet, Sanskrit, Aramaic, and Latin. This has its merit and there is a different type of power that is instilled into words that have been treated as holy and sacred by thousands and thousands of people over a long period of time. Consider the following words: Amen, Adonai, Tetragrammaton, Yahweh, Ateh, Malkuth, Ve Geburah, Ve Gedullah, Le Olam... these are all holy words that have power amplified within them due to thousands of years of use as an esoteric and sacred language.

The issue with foreign language, regardless of how sacred it might be, is one of comprehension and focus. If the person who uses the words understands fully what they mean and uses that meaning within their energy work, then the words become a process that help facilitate the flow of energy and even amplify it. If, however, the person is distracted by whether or not their pronunciation will be correct, if they do not know the true meaning or correct usage of the word, and if the language is only used it for flash and show, then it is likely to be a detriment to the successful flow of energy.

God loves an educated person who uses their knowledge artfully in communication. God does not appreciate a show off.

Just as there is tremendous power in the written word and the spoken word, there is also a specific energy in silence. The Wiccans have a lovely dictate called The Witch's Pyramid, which goes like this:

> To
> Know
> To Dare
> To Will &
> To Be Silent

This is a beautiful demonstration of the power of self-control. "To Know" means to know when to act and when to be still. "To Dare" means to be brave enough to act when it is necessary and not just worry a situation to death or doubt yourself into paralysis. "To will" means to have the conviction of truth and good intent and "make it so." "To Be Silent" means that once you have done your energy work, you do not talk it to death and bleed away all of the energy from the process. There are times when working quietly and keeping your own counsel is the best course of action.

Runes and symbols are another form of communication and language that both the Higher Self and the Conscious Self understand. The use of symbols and simple pictures speaks to both Selves simultaneously and helps them to coordinate their efforts. If we show the average person a simple picture of a sun:

...most people will have both their Higher Self and

Conscious Self process the image of "Sun." This is because there is not only a long-standing, historical agreement that yes indeed, that is a drawing of a sun, but also because we have a current social understanding that yes, that is a sun.

If we show the average person a pentacle, on the other hand:

...the Higher Self of most people will react to the definition ingrained in their DNA's collective consciousness and interpret it as, "a spiritual symbol representing the elements of Earth, Air, Fire, Water, and Spirit draw together by a unifying circle." Thousands of years of conditioning of the Higher Self will cause it to react to the traditional meaning of the symbol.

The Conscious Self of many people, however, will override the Higher Self and say, "No! Shut up! You are wrong! That is a symbol of the Devil!" Their social conditioning that is born of a relatively short amount of time can counteract thousands of years of historical programming.

The use of symbols in Bio-Universal energy work, as we are sure you can see, is a matter of finding the symbols that YOUR Higher Self and Conscious Self are in accordance over the meaning and using them as a gateway to one another and a language they both speak. Once you do, it is easier to connect to Higher Self by simply using symbols or colors or other forms of language common to both selves.

Creating a Common Group Goal

There is absolutely no way to convey the impact of concerted group focus in the process of manifestation. Prayer chains the world over are dedicated specifically to the act of harnessing group energy and directing it toward a common goal. People gather for worship in churches, synagogues, groves, and circles to share the sacred experience and enhance the power of worship.

If you study the principles of force, inertia, and friction, you know that when we apply force to an object, we generate a particular energy referred to as a Newton after Sir Isaac Newton who pioneered the study of this effect. Imagine a car needs to be pushed a particular distance. If two people apply force to the car, the number of Newtons is doubled. If three apply force, the number of Newton's is tripled. Each time more Newtons are added, the car becomes easier to move.

The same principle applies to the "force" you use to push your own Bio-Universal energy toward its goal. If you need money to pay your rent and you center up, pull up your own bio-energy, connect in with God and feel the Universal energy flowing, mix them together into a happy energy cocktail, amplify them with some incense made with herbs and oils that are good for drawing in money, burn a green candle to bring in the focus of money and send your will out into the ether, you will likely get a good result. You are using many different complimentary actions to speed up the energy moving toward your goal.

The more people you add to the concentrated focus on your goal, the greater the flow of energy and the better the result. Engaging a group in directing Bio-Universal energy toward a common goal is a tremendous asset to the process.

Can you do it on your own? Absolutely and without a doubt. If you can do it with a group, however, the results are much stronger provided the entire group has good focus on the desired outcome and wants the same result.

Astrological Influences & Timing

Earlier in this book, we talked about how throughout our lives, we learn the most advantageous times to use our energy to get what we want quickly and more easily. This premise applies strongly in Bio-Universal energy work because of the characteristics of the different Sun and Moon placements in astrology.

Assigned to them by people over the ages, the planets, the moon, and the sun all have a particular energy to them. The Sun is strong, aggressive, and omnipresent. This caused people over time to think of it as a masculine energy. The moon is elusive, cyclic, and mysterious. These qualities caused people to think of it as feminine.

As the Moon and the Sun move through their cycles of the month and year, the energy that they give forth will change. These changes plus the energy that results from the position of the Sun and Moon in relation to one another and the planets creates the foundations of astrology. For our own purposes, we mostly consider how those heavenly bodies move in relation to our position on Earth. This information can certainly be a tremendous asset to our energy flow if we learn how they influence our daily life.

The phase of the moon, for instance, lends the energy of the cycle of new beginnings, fruition, and banishment. The New Moon period is a time of growth and fresh starts. Waxing Moon is a good time to begin actions and work toward adding to your life in some way. Full Moon is a time of fruition and fullness. Waning Moon is a time to work toward what you would like to have leave your life and diminish in power or importance.

We can phrase nearly all goals in such a way as to use the energy of the moon phase in which you are working. For instance, if our goal is to lose weight, we believe we cannot move forward with this goal if it is a New Moon. New Moons are for gaining, not for losing! We can ask, however, for will power, good health, a strong and vibrant body, greater self-esteem, etc. If we wish to work for wealth and prosperity but it is a Full Moon, we can banish poverty and lack. Just turn your wishes inside out and rephrase them to fit the Moon cycle.

The Sun cycles, however, take us through the entirety of the year, allowing us to use certain historical power days to create long-term manifestation of bigger projects and goals. Most people inherently understand that there is a very different energy to the season of spring (new beginnings) than to fall (endings). Our books *The Little Book of Days and Times of Power*, *The Little Book of Real Magic*, and *CUSP* go into extensive detail of how to use the eight power days of the ancient agricultural year to manifest positive long term changes in our lives. Since these ancient holidays were honored over thousands of years as we emerged and developed as an agricultural society, we have the trigger of those days embedded into our collective consciousness. We automatically react to their call and using their energies to bring about our own "harvests" in our lives is an extremely proactive and rewarding process.

Stones

People often laugh at "New Agers" for using quartz crystals as tools of focus. When you hold quartz in your hand and focus your energy through it, it regulates the flow of energy through your body and, if you hold the crystal correctly, *out of your body* and toward a goal. That is why wands, which are tools used to project energy toward a specific target, often have quartz crystal at the far end. That may sound silly until you consider that very, very tiny quartz crystals are used to regulate the energy of what? Time itself. Watches. Watches are some of the most intricate constructions mankind has ever invented and a tiny crystal regulates the pulses of energy inside it. If the properties of quartz enable it to regulate energy in a watch, why would it then not also regulate the pulses of energy in your body and from your body?

Hematite is a silvery, shiny, magnetic stone. It is named as it is for its ability to pull impurities out of the bloodstream and discharge negative energy from the body. Shakespeare said, "There are more things in heaven and earth, Horatio, than are dreamt of in your philosophy." There are so many things on this earth that we do not understand. The beauty is that we do not have to understand them to gain the benefits of them. God exists in all things, all through nature, and this being the case, there is divine energy that is inherent in stones, herbs, and other natural structures. The bits of energy living in these items, waiting to be released, are like special gifts from God to boost our personal energy.

You can put stones with the qualities you wish to invoke out on your hearth or your dresser, you can carry them in your pocket or against your body. You can even put them into a little mojo bag with other items that are sympathetic to your goals (items you consider sacred, herbs that help your cause, etc) and then carry or wear the bag.

There are many online and printed references regarding the magical properties of gemstones, common stones, and minerals. Any of these will be useful to you in using stones to boost the energy of our work.

Weather

Of all of the factors we could discuss that amp up magical energy, for Katrina, there is nothing like a good rainstorm. From the smell of those first few drops hitting parched land to the thunder and lightning all the way through the rivers of water running down the road, rain wakes up her Higher Self in a big way. A friend of ours is terrified of thunderstorms and tries to sleep until they are over. Katrina is the one running out into the middle of typhoons (literally), electrical storms, and hurricanes trying to tap that natural energy. She feels the power of Nature and God in those moments where others feel fear or inconvenience.

Eric, on the other hand, feels most alive with the sun beating down hard on him in the summer days, relaxing on his boat with the lake breeze in his face. To him, the power of the Sun is a vibrant expression of God and the strength of male energy.

A warm spring day is magical with the earth softening from the grip of winter, a soft breeze carrying the scent of daffodils and the promise of new beginnings. A snowstorm outside and a fire in the fireplace are magical to some. Each person has their weather "triggers" that make them blossom with energy.

We all have our special metrological times and should take full advantage of them when they occur. Sensory experiences that we can see, smell, hear, feel, and taste are some of the strongest motivators of the human psyche and will greatly assist with the working of magical energy.

Our book *The Little Book of Weather Witchery* covers extensively weather and the energy inherent in different types of climate and weather. *The Little Book of Days and Times of Power* covers solar and lunar moments that amplify magical energy.

Visual Cues

Humans respond very strongly, sometimes at a visceral and subconscious level, to what they see in front of them. When a Catholic person prays the Rosary, they use the beads as a focus tool that they can see and touch as they pray. When a person misses someone they love, they will often hold an article of clothing that smells like the person they miss and acts as a visual reminder of a time when they were not apart. We keep photos of our loved ones on our walls and our mantles and in our wallets to evoke a feeling when we see them.

There are many, many techniques for creating harmonious energy around us. Honoring the four natural elements in each room is a good start. Create a special place for earth, air, fire, and water in your rooms. This does not have to be elaborate. A shell can suffice for water, a stone for earth, a feather for air, and a candle for fire. Many books on creating a magical home are available. Of the most notable is Scott Cunningham's, *The Magical Household.*

Haunt thrift stores, yard sales, and second hand shops for unusual statues and obscure paintings that awaken your spirit and send it soaring into the stars. Never be afraid to nurture yourself in this way. The more you work to create a sacred environment around you all of the time, the more connected, fulfilled, and happy you will be. This in turn will cause you to radiate joy, Bio-Universal energy, and light. Truly, nourishing your aesthetic delights is a service to those around you, assisting you in showing them your very best self.

It is difficult to cultivate a holy and sacred vibe in a room or house that is disorderly, dirty, and full of stale air.

Regarding your actual energy work, visual cues are very important for pulling in your focus to the target. Wish boards and goal boards are a lovely way to amplify your energy toward a goal. Pictures of your goal fulfilled and representations of where you want to be when the process is over are powerful tools.

If you are directing your magical energy to a specific person for protection, healing, or other work, a photo of the person is a nice point of focus. You can light candles around the picture or highlight it in some other way. Basically, anything that assists you in feeling connected to the work you are doing and amplifies the energy you are able to generate toward that work is a great addition.

Now that we have covered some of the ways that you can speed up your Bio-Universal energy flow, let's talk about some of the factors that can slow down or totally derail your energy flow.

Chapter 4 - What Slows Down Bio-Universal Energy Flow?

If we consider Newton's laws of physics, we know that friction is what resists motion. The law of inertia says that once an object is in motion, it will tend to stay in motion until a force acts upon it and slows it down or stops it. This applies to energy as well, including Bio-Universal energy. Energy continues until something slows it down or stops it. What we want, of course, is for our energy to move swiftly toward our goal with the strongest charge possible.

When performing Bio-Universal energy work, it pays to know what causes energy to slow down or ground itself. What causes our energy work efforts to "fail" or take longer? It's very true that not every prayer is answered and not every effort is successful in terms of what the intention of the person was at the time it was enacted. If we know what can ground our energy and interfere with the connection, so to speak, we can sometimes avoid those pitfalls or at least better understand them when they occur.

The Influence of Fate and the Greatest Good

As we have taught Bio-Universal energy classes over the

past many years, we have had many students ask us about the influence of fate on our "proactive prayer," as we have sometimes called magical work. What happens when God/The Universe/Goddess says, "No?" We cannot begin to count the number of energy work processes we have done with tremendously pure intent only to never have our goal manifest. Every single time this happened, even though we did not get what we wanted, we usually got something better or were able to see why another path was better for us than the one we wanted.

In our arrogance, we assume we know exactly what is best for our lives and will sometimes even beg, plead, and wrestle with God over our own greatest good. This will most assuredly slow down positive results. It is a similar experience as a good parent who has a child who is throwing a tantrum because they cannot have or do what they want. The child wants to eat a huge bag of candy all at once or play in the street or go to the party with no adults present and the parent says, "No, that's not going to happen." The child does not have the experience, maturity, or long-term vision to understand why the parent is stopping the happy parade. All the child knows is that they cannot have what they want and they are angry. In retrospect, with the benefit of greater knowledge, wisdom, and the passage of time, they are able better understand why it was a bad idea to fly off the roof pretending to be Superman.

As rational, reasonable adults, we make choices for our

lives based on what we know at the time to be true. Our vision, however, is limited to our own previous experiences, as well as what we can see before us and around us at any given time. This Higher Power we call God, however, can see where we need to be for our own greatest good and works to direct us there. Most of the time, our efforts invested into Bio-Universal energy work do not take us off track from our ultimate divine purpose. Sometimes, however, what we work to create would cause an unnecessary diversion that could delay or greatly limit our progress. Others may even take us into dangerous situations that we cannot foresee from our current vantage point. Those destructive situations are the efforts that God will thwart.

Sometimes, what you want is simply not meant to be and the reason it is not meant to be is purely for your own protection and ultimate fulfillment. When you fully and completely trust that one premise, you have mastered the process.

If your energy work does not divert you from the Higher Purpose of your life, then it will likely take hold if your intent is pure and you connect in on a strong level. If you are working for a condition that will take you away from your higher life purpose and interfere with what will ultimately bring you satisfaction and joy, then it is likely your energy will ground out and neutralized.

The Influence of Free Will

One of the universal standards in ethical behavior is that you never perform Bio-Universal energy work that manipulates the free will of another person. For instance, you do not ask the Universe to "make" someone love you if he or she does not have those feelings. You do not ask that someone to leave their home or job if you know that is not their desire. This is practical as well as ethical because the power of a person's free will is very strong. It takes a tremendous amount of personal energy to overcome the free will of another and manipulate their life. This degree of energy is also normally not sustainable, so the effect would not last very long. Typically, such manipulation is NOT in our own greatest good anyway and would ground and neutralize. The point of using Bio-Universal energy is to work on yourself and your own life; not someone else's.

If your goal involves other people, make certain that you are phrasing you goal in such a way that the impact of the result is on *you* rather than on others. If you want to manifest a romantic relationship, do not center your work on one person, but rather work toward a particular way you want to feel in a relationship and a certain type of relationship you desire. If you want a better paying job, do not work toward taking someone else's job, but instead work toward how you want to feel in your new job and the details of the job you wish to have. This also opens up more options for the Universe to bring you what you want rather than limiting its focus on one particular situation.

One of the fastest ways your energy grounds is by your own free will getting in the way. Let's say you don't have a job and you know you really need one and if you don't get one, you're going to be in a serious financial lurch. You engage Bio-Universal energy to get a job, but you want to stay home in bed and not go to work. If your entire will is not behind the energy you send to your goal, your energy will be divided and weakened. It is important that you do the homework, so to speak, and clear away any internal obstacles you may have to your success. Maybe you ask that a relationship be healed when that really is not what you want. You might ask to attract buyers to your house when deep down, you do not want to move. Free will choices will not always derail your energy work, but they can most certainly slow it down.

Another way that Free Will has a major impact on magical endeavors is in the practice of gambling. One would think it would be easy to go to a slot machine, roulette wheel, or a card table send some energy toward the cards or the wheel and pour out a jackpot. The problem with gambling, especially lotteries, is that you are placing your free will choices up against those of many others who all want the target just as much as you do. The free will of all of those people pulls against and balances out your own free will interests. The free will desires of the casino are also at play. In short, gambling is one of the very few completely neutral places where if a win is meant to be, it will happen.

Lack of Cohesion

God is very forgiving and knows your heart before you speak your will. Your presentation of your intention, goal, or wish is to only amplify your own part of the energy boost and clarify to yourself exactly what you want to have happen. In the previous section, we talked about the importance of making sure that your entire being is behind the intention you put forward rather than some part of yourself pulling in a different direction. Bio-Universal energy flows best when your intent is clear and focused and your environment is supportive and calm.

If you get your ritual area all set up and believe that you are ready to go and things start to fall apart, it is time to pay attention. You light your correctly colored candles and the dog knocks over a plant in the next room. You center up and prepare to court your Higher Self and your child, who you thought was sleeping, wakes up and needs attention. You come back to find that your candles went out and you have to relight them. After you get the candles lit, someone knocks at the door... and so it goes.

During those inevitable times when you find that despite your best efforts, your ritual seems to be falling apart around you, it is critical that you stop and recognize what is happening rather than continuing to attempt to "herd the cats."

If one or two things trip you up, that is not normally cause for concern. If you experience a greater number of interfering factors, then it may be a message or "redirect," as we call them. Usually, we are being told by The Universe that it is not yet time for us to do the work we were about to enact. Why? Here are some possible causes:

> *The proposed outcome was inappropriate for reasons we do not yet know (or we do and we are ignoring).*
>
> *We need more information before proceeding*
>
> *We should reconsidered and reframe our ritual. Something is off.*
>
> *Energies are already in motion toward your goal and further attempts would be wasted effort. (Usually, this will not slow you down, but we have known it to happen)*

As humans, we very much want to believe that we know what is best at any given time and often cannot imagine that we may not have the full picture. Humility and grace are valuable tools in Bio-Universal energy work. It is helpful to heed the gentle nudges from the Universe. These help us to tune into the flow of natural progression with a much cleaner and stronger signal.

If you choose to continue with your energy work despite The Universe's attempt to curtail your efforts, you probably will not bring about Armageddon. It is more likely that your energy will ground and neutralize or you will not obtain optimal results. Our advice is that it is better to stop what you are doing, wait a few hours while you re-evaluate your approach, then try again from a different angle at a different time. Often, the reason for the delay or change will be revealed as time goes on.

Physical Discomfort/Illness

Distraction is one of the fastest ways for your energy to lose speed and you will notice that many of the obstacles to good energy flow that we learn about in this book have an element of distraction to them. Focus is important and the more of your attention you can commit to the Bio-Universal energy process, the better your results will be.

Physical discomfort can be a tremendous distraction and have quite an impact on your ability to focus. In church, some people find hard pews and kneeling stools to be uncomfortable. In Pagan circles, working outside is often far, far too cold in the later months. Headaches, cramps, sinus problems and other maladies can all work to rob you of precious focus and energy. When most people are ill, their body energies focus naturally on the healing process and energy reserves that are normally available for bio-energy use are otherwise engaged. It takes even more energy to pull them away from the healing they are attempting to facilitate and go outward into a magical direction, not to mention that your healing is not getting the energy it needs.

It is hard to feel magical if your feet are stinging from being cold or you are sweltering and can feel your skin burning in the sun. Making certain that you are as physically comfortable as possible is a big part of protecting your energy resources for ritual time to achieve optimum energy output.

Another aspect of physical comfort is fatigue. It is no secret that fatigue will affect both our physical energy levels and our ability for rational thought. People use sleep deprivation as a form of torture! Performing effective Bio-Universal energy work when you are sleep-compromised and exhausted is almost impossible. Make certain that you feel well rested, centered, and physically comfortable when it comes time for your energy work.

High Emotion/Hormonal Shifts

Emotion is a big part of what drives your own bio-energy because it is at the heart of what you want to have happen. If you cannot feel then you cannot want. High emotion of all kinds: love, fear, sadness, anger, frustration, etc., can and will fuel your energy like a stoked furnace.

On the other hand, high emotion can also occasionally render us unreasonable and irrational. It is completely up to the person to determine whether they are in a mentally stable place to approach energy work. The biggest question regarding high emotion is motivation and intent. If you are using your energy to create a positive outcome for yourself or others, then that is a pure intent. If you are using your energy to get revenge on someone else, that is not a good time to go into ritual.

Hormonal shifts can play with our emotions and cause us to have unbalanced reactions to situations, even causing us to believe we want things we do not normally want. This is true for both males and females. It is best to go into a working energy ritual with a level head, but full of strong intent fueled by positive emotion. That positive emotion can take the form of "hope" if the current situation is challenging. Certainly, you do not have to live in a world of rainbows, puppy dogs, and roses to effectively use Bio-Universal energy. For optimum results, however, you should always make certain that when you go into ritual, you are pure of intent and are thinking clearly. For this reason, it is usually not advised that a person go into ritual if they are intoxicated.

Smells

You know, it sounds simple. It is not. A major distraction and energy drain can take hold if the area where you are working stinks...literally. A common smell that hosts may not notice they have – but their guests surely will - is that of animal odors. People who live in an area with animals become habituated to the smells of their pets. For people who do not live there, however, dog, cat, snake, or rodent smells can be overwhelming. We have participated in group rituals where the smell of a cat box was so overpowering our eyes burned. The ammonia was thick in the air. To say we were distracted and had difficulty focusing on the magical work at hand is quite an understatement. Odors are not limited to animals. Tobacco smells, trash, body odor, and spoiled food can be just as distracting. What smells good or does not is highly subjective and not always related to cleanliness. Some people hate the smell of certain incenses or herbs that may be burning.

Make sure your working area is lovely and that there are no distracting smells.

Psychic Vampires/Black Holes

We are sure you have had experiences where you walk away from spending time with someone, even someone you like or love, and just felt drained. Some people are exhausting. Some people are needy and just pull the energy right out of you. Some people are contentious and argumentative and even those who loves a good debate can get weary from it after a while. Psychic vampires suck away your energy, which leaves less for you to direct toward your goal.

It can be difficult to avoid those people who are energy black holes if they are in your family or work environment. We strongly advise that if you are going to do Bio-Universal energy work, stay clear of these kinds of people for several hours before you begin. You need your energy for you and the work you are doing. You should not pour it away needlessly.

Ideally, as you create a life that is responsible and energy centered, you will find ways to distance yourself from these types of people so that your energy level remains optimum.

Clutter, Chatter, Chaos

You absolutely do not have to be a neat freak to work effective with Bio-Universal energy. Your environment does not have to be sterile and squeaky clean. It does help tremendously to have a ritual area that is free of clutter and chaos. Our minds register everything we see in our immediate environment and the more there is to see, the busier we get trying to see it. That is an energy bleed.

When we are working with Bio-Universal energy, ideally everything we see would make us feel empowered and magical. If our eyes have to see piles and piles of clutter and stuff everywhere, it is harder for the magical items to pop and register in our minds. All we see is "stuff."

If no other place in your house is clutter-free, your

energy working area should at least be nicely organized and attractive. Your mind should be able to focus on the task at hand; not forty or fifty other things you should be doing. Clutter distracts our minds and pulls our focus away from the energy we direct.

Under this category, we would also include distracting sounds. Again, your need is to focus intently and that is hard to do with a jackhammer pounding outside your window, dogs barking, music blaring from another room, people shouting upstairs, and a phone ringing. It is essential that you reduce all the distractions you can manage before you begin your energy work. Clear away the sound clutter as well as the visual clutter.

Metal Jewelry

Metal is a material that holds energy very well. Some people react with discomfort to buying used jewelry, feeling there was bad energy stored in it. There are several simple processes to cleanse out metal objects and clear away any negative energy.

Other people, however, find that different metals ground their energy. We have known folks who had to remove all rings, earrings, and bracelets before they worked in order to get the maximum energy push. This appears to be very individual and can even change throughout a person's life. Experiment and see if you are sensitive to metals in terms of your energy generating abilities. Some jewelry, particularly those with precious stones, can actually amplify your energy instead of grounding it.

Metal, by nature, is an excellent conductor of energy and so in theory, it should amplify, not ground energy. If you find that you are sensitive, see if it is to all metal or just particular items. There may be energies inherent in those items that are at work tapping out your own personal energy. It is a very interesting course of study and can assist you in managing your energy levels mundanely as well as magically.

Worry or Lack of Faith

Often, students have contacted us saying that they did energy work for a specific outcome and now they wonder if they should do more magic to give it a boost. What they are saying is that they have not yet seen evidence that their energy work took hold and they are questioning whether they did it correctly or had enough energy to make it really fly. They doubt themselves or they doubt that God heard and will reply.

There are some magical efforts that are specifically set up to be performed in multiple sessions. If you want a "wave" effect that boosts the energy over time, you can plan your energy process to work exactly that way. In this case, however, we are talking about questioning and doubting the process you followed.

As we have mentioned before, The Universe knows your heart and intention before you speak it or work magic toward it. The work we do is to honor the universal energies and to amplify our own personal energy to invest toward the goal. If you did it with good energy and purity of intention, you did it right.

Once you have engaged the Bio-Universal energies in an act of magic toward a specific goal, the most productive step you can take is to walk away from it knowing it was a job well done. If it does not bear fruit, then you have to believe that for whatever reason, it was not meant to be or was not meant to be right now. God does not only say, "No." Sometimes, God simply says, "Not yet." Regardless, God always says, "Don't worry. I've got this."

If you planted a seed, you would not go back a couple of weeks later to dig it up and see if it is growing. To do so would kill the very process you are trying to cultivate. Instead, you nourish it and wait patiently for signs of life. In magic, you do the same. Plant you seed and have faith that it will flourish into a garden of success and greatest good. That is the truest nature of putting your trust in The Universe. Make your will known, put your energy toward it, and then have the courage, conviction, and faith to walk away confident that it will be accomplished if it is for the greatest good.

Chapter 5 – In Summary

Life happens. We cannot control everything in our environment and should not seek to do so. We are, however, clearly responsible for our own happiness and primarily our own choices and reactions to circumstances bring us to where we land in life. Most people find that they want to exist in a joyful, happy life that is free of drama, worry, and fear. Too often, we place that happiness on hold until…

> ***Until we lose weight.***
>
> ***Until we find the right romantic partner.***
>
> ***Until we until we make a particular amount of money.***
>
> ***Until we live in a particular style of house.***
>
> ***Until we have children.***
>
> ***Until we do not have children.***
>
> ***Until we retire.***
>
> ***Until we are dead.***

For most people, there is a list of at least 5-6 things, the absence of which is robbing them from experiencing true happiness. From that point, the picture becomes more grim because then we get into the type of people who do not have their handful of happiness tokens and it is someone else's fault. Next, we get the type people who do not have their happiness tokens because of someone else and they are very, very angry about it. After that comes those who do not have their happiness tokens AND it is someone else's fault AND they are very, very angry about it AND they are not going to let a soul forget it.

When we look at any of those objective alternatives, we think we can all agree that we do not want to be that person. We want to be the person who is joyful and happy every day, regardless of what comes into their life or does not. The only way that experience occurs (and we are not being extreme in saying *"the only way that occurs"*) is when we accept full accountability for what happens in our lives and conversely, accept the power to change what does not work for us. Accountability itself gives us power and ends the victim mentality that leaves so many of us paralyzed and unable to progress.

You saw one common word that started each of those conditions above that many people use to forestall their own happiness: *Until.* Our suggestion is to use that word as an empowerment rather than a hindrance and assign a stop date to its influence. Change your thinking to use the phrase: *"Until NOW."* Those are two of the most powerful words you will ever encounter because they mark a distinct delineation between two forms of behavior:

"Until NOW, I did this..." "Now, I do this..."

"Until now..." gives you the power of change in two simple words. The difference between a dream and a goal is a target date.

Decide what you want to have different in your life a week, a month, or a year from now. Write it out in as much detail as you can imagine and work through any feeling of resistance in your head. It will sound like, *"But obviously that can't happen..."* and *"So and so is NOT going to like this!"* and *"Who do you think you are being so selfish?"*

Simply see your goal as a reality in your mind, imagine how you will feel when it is happening, and write it out. You do not have to see how you will get there; only the end result. While you do this, shut down the drama queen in your head who persists in insisting that it will not and cannot happen. Over time, that voice will do what other voices do that clamor for attention and do not get it. It will be quiet.

Go down the list of factors that speed up your energy in relation to that particular goal. Love? Pink or red love? Bloodstone or rose quartz? Rose hips, maybe? Listening to Bryan Adams or Richard Marx songs on loop until you trance out? Are friends sick to death of hearing you whine about being alone? Invite them over to help you raise energy toward your goal! (Clean your cat box and take out the trash first.) Everything you learned in this book will give you another little boost of energy to add to your process.

Blessed be.

About The Authors

Katrina Rasbold has provided insightful and guidance to countless individuals over the past three decades through both her life path consultations and her informative classes and workshops. She has worked with teachers all over the world, including three years of training in England and two years of practice in the Marianas Islands. She is a professional life coach who holds a PhD in Religion.

Eric Rasbold is a lifelong student of philosophy, spiritualism and religious theology. He is a Gulf War Veteran and avid gold miner. His degree is in business and he is a licensed electrical contractor working in the solar energy industry.

Eric and Katrina are co-owners of the Botánica de La

Reina in Roseville, California where they sell the magical items they make by hand and help people through Bio-Universal energy work.

Since 1997, Eric Rasbold and Katrina have created, developed, lived and now written of the philosophy and practice of the spiritual path known as Climbing Up The Spiral Pathway that has been enjoyed and celebrated by thousands wishing to take an active role in changing the course of their lives and improving their connection with the Divine. In addition to the main practice, they have also developed a complete series that teaches the ways and means of effective union of the body, mind and spirit through the responsible and ethical use of Energy Magic and Bio-Universal energies.

Eric and Katrina live in the forested Eden of the High Sierras of Northern California near Tahoe. Eric enjoys all outdoor activities that will allow communion with nature, especially in places that are not often frequented by people. They both frequently teach workshops on different aspects of Bio-Universal energy usage in the El Dorado, Sacramento, and Placer counties of California, as well as Pantheacon in San Jose, California. They have six children, two teens at home and four who are grown up and out there loose in the world.

Other Books by the Authors

How to Be a Queen

Where the Daffodils Grow

The Daughters of Avalon

Rose of Avalon

The Dance Card

Energy Magic

Energy Magic Compleat

Beyond Energy Magic

CUSP

Properties of Magical Energy

Reuniting the Two Selves

Magical Ethics and Protection

The Art of Ritual Crafting

The Magic and Making of Candles and Soaps

Days and Times of Power

Crossing The Third Threshold

How to Create a Magical Working Group

An Insider's Guide to the General Hospital Fan Club Weekend

Leaving Kentucky in the Broad Daylight

The Real Magic

Get Your Book Published

Goddess in the Kitchen: The Magic and Making of Food

Spiritual Childbirth

Tarot For Real People

Weather or Not

Weather Witchery

Spiritual Childbirth

Made in the USA
Middletown, DE
21 April 2022